THE LITTLE BLUE BOOK OF LIMERICKS

KEVIN LUCAS

For permission requests, write to the publisher at:
"Attention: Permissions Coordinator"
Temptation Press
PO Box 1172
Union Lake, Michigan 48387
mailto:info@TemptationPress.com

Published in the United States by Temptation Press
http://www.TemptationPress.com
All Rights Reserved

© 2018 Kevin Lucas

Tradepaper ISBN: 978-1-947210-10-3
Kindle ISBN: 978-1-947210-11-0
Digital ISBN: 978-1-947210-12-7
Library of Congress Control Number: 2017961296

First Edition: January 2018

TEMPTATION
PRESS

THE LITTLE BLUE BOOK OF LIMERICKS

KEVIN LUCAS

DEDICATION

To my wife Terri, who brings out the naughty in me.

ACKNOWLEDGEMENTS

There are too many people to thank for the honed limericks you will read in these pages. I would, however, like to acknowledge four people who have helped immensely in this fine-tuning process—Chris J. Strolin, Joanna Keene, Jesse Frankovich, and Janet McConnaughey.

Thank you.

Edward Lear, that famed Brit of droll mind,
Gave us limericks (light verses, five-lined).
But the type I like sharin'
Are rooted in Erin,
The lewd and lascivious kind.

Two junior high girls, buddy-buddy,
Were innocent, carefree, and nutty.
But separate paths taken
Meant friendship forsaken.
One's wholesome; the other turned slutty.

In the Garden of Eden one night,
Horny Eve, with no fig leaf in sight,
Asked, "You wanna give in
To that sweet taste of sin?"
Exclaimed Adam, enamored, "I'll bite!"

There once was a gambler who said,
"When a woman gets into my bed,
Then that's pretty good odds
That she wants to join bods.
I proceed, thus, to cover the spread."

"From *emotion, emote* came to be;
Burglar—burgle; from *pease* we got *pea*,"
Said a co-ed, none cuter,
Who's acting as tutor.
Back formations she's doing with me.

The minister's daughter is barred
From a boy she holds high in regard;
But the prayers that her dad
Makes her say only add
To her lust, 'cause they're long, and they're hard.

Receiving a sexual guide,
An assumed inexperienced bride
And groom laughed as they wrote
To the senders a note—
"These positions we've already tried."

A nurse, nearly blind, caused some harm
At a nudist camp blood drive, alarm-
ing a man with a penis
So huge and so venous,
The nurse truly thought it his arm.

Said a virgin, "I'd like to abstain
From premarital sex." "Why refrain?"
Asked the guy she was dating.
They were later caught mating
At Bob's Quickie Chapel on Main.

"I'd like to put brains on display
With you guys, but my boobs have a way
To distract, interfere
With my mind; that's up here."
"Oh, I'm sorry. Uh, what did you say?"

In a Mackinac courtroom, a judge
Told me, "Son, your small crime's just a smudge,
So community service."
But *that* makes me nervous—
He says I'll assist packing fudge.

On my sex doll, each cranny I checked;
Anatomically, she is correct.
She's so totally there,
Womb and ovary pair,
That a kid in nine months I expect.

The class laughed and called Mary a fool.
The teacher explained, "As a rule,
If safe sex is your quest,
Latex condoms are best,
Not those lambskins you brought into school."

Eddie Haskell's an overachiever
With cajolery toward Mrs. Cleaver.
With his gentle, repeated
Appeals, he's succeeded
In getting along with the beaver.

From the rooms, I could hear all the moans.
"Just the basics," I told Madam Jones.
"I don't want any frills."
So she offered the skills
Of the newbie, stripped down to bare bones.

A dentist is facing the gravity
Of his infamous acts of depravity.
He was taken to court
On a woman's report
Of him trying to fill the wrong cavity.

A playboy, a bit on the wild side,
Conjoined with a gal on the mild side.
She said, "Don't wear a glove,"
'Cause she thought it was love,
But it wasn't. She later, with child, sighed.

Don't look now, but your wife's over there
At the bar. You can glance, but don't stare;
She may see and infer
That we're spying on her.
Ain't that chick she just tongued your au pair?

Jack chased Jill up the hill, and he caught her.
They fell down to the ground, and he brought her
To orgasmic delight
As he thrusted up tight.
Nine months subsequent, Jill broke her water.

Said a virgin, exceedingly purty,
"My folks raised me not to be flirty."
One day, her sweet smile meant
A nighttime defilement;
With chasteness erased, she's now "dirty."

We played bridge with some friends; no command
Did we have, so we played our own brand
In the bedroom that night.
She played south; with delight,
I went north. She'd an excellent hand!

A shy call girl, not getting a mob
Of rich clients to shell out a gob
Of their money, was told
Some advice good as gold—
It's best to lie down on the job.

A guy met a nympho and, struck
By her beauty, he thought, "I'm in luck."
He asked if she'd go
All the way. She said, "No.
For you, sir, I don't give a fuck."

I auditioned on harp, a so-so job.
Judged only on that, I'd have no job.
In my dogged pursuit,
I auditioned on flute.
The conductor then gave me a blow job.

The person most loyal is dear
Mrs. Claus, who sheds many a tear
Because Santa's sex drive
Is just barely alive.
He only comes one time a year.

My wife's a cold fish in our bed.
She's aloof, and her passion is dead.
So, unable to please her,
I went to the freezer
And warmed up the salmon instead.

All these co-eds are cute, but I'm shy.
"Make the effort," my friend said. "Say hi.
The man who is wussy
Won't get any pussy,
So give it the old college try."

Thought a strict Catholic girl, "Heaven knows
That my principles bar giving blows;
But I wonder if maybe a
Few licks of my labia
Could get me to compromise those."

A whore told a guy that men paid her
Good money to orally cater.
He then gave it a try,
But her client said, "I
Like fellatrixes. Save it, fellator."

There once was a john with a thirst
For the consummate hooker—well-versed
In the sexual deed.
Then he found one whose creed
Was "The customer always comes first."

An intercourse study was done
Showing women encounter more fun
Screwing men with two phalluses.
Here's the analysis—
Two heads are better than one.

Mary Magdalene used to go chumming
With all of the guys. Now they're bumming
'Cause she chose from the men
One who's risen again.
She experienced Christ's second coming.

Said my date after viewing my pole,
"I'm sorry for quashing your goal
Of getting some action
With me, but your fraction
Is simply too small for my hole."

There once was a eunuch enthralled
By a beautiful woman. Forestalled
Was a joining of hearts
When she learned of the parts
That he lacked—she liked men who were balled.

Into bed I was hoping to leap
With a knockout anesthetist. Deep
Was my interest, I thought,
But it all was for nought
On our date when she put me to sleep.

A self-described virgin, a fox,
Is a hit with us guys—she sucks cocks.
But how could that be,
One might ask, to which she
Would say, "Try thinking outside the box."

Avid sperm bank contributor, Merv
Is thought selfless. They cryopreserve
His donations in sub-
zero temps. Here's the rub—
Merv, in fact, is a whacking-off perv.

You can get there with passion or not.
Doesn't matter. I'm horny and hot,
So come take me. All roads
Lead to Rome; different modes
Will achieve the same goal. *That's the spot!*

I thought she referred to my dong,
But I found my assumption was wrong.
Seems I failed to excite,
And she looked to take flight.
She remarked, "It's just so-so. So long."

A woman with barely a cent,
Yet who lives on her own, is intent
On providing her muff
To her landlord to stuff—
This in lieu of her paying the rent.

Contrary is Mary, that gal.
In her garden, she'll grow your morale.
Though that belle's mind is pretty
Made up to show titty,
Your cock'll be teased; yes, it shall.

A hooker in court had a worry
A judge might convict in a hurry.
For twelve men, she did pray.
She lucked out, as did they.
In their room, she was tried by the jury.

Every night we want sex, without fail.
Different kinds, though, so who will prevail?
A coin flip will tell us.
Tonight I feel jealous—
No head. I'll be giving her tail.

I had asked, "Do you wanna cavort?"
She replied, "A day late, dollar short.
He asked first." I won't pout.
I don't mind missing out
Since I learned of her genital wart.

An old woman who lived in a shoe,
An ex-hooker, had many a screw.
She made lots of bread
In her infamous bed.
She made lots of children there too.

A sexual catalog listed
A plug-in device for assisted
Release of guys' spurts,
But the price really hurts.
Call me stingy—I'm staying close-fisted.

Said a virgin in heat, "Get to shovin'
It in, 'cause I knead some good lovin'."
He defloured her there,
Giving rise to a prayer—
That he gave her no bun in the oven.

Your ex-flame says the chances are greater
Than lesser that you, when you laid her,
Impregnated her.
The paternity's sure—
You're Luke's baby daddy, Darth Vader.

You can yank all you want, but of course,
I must tell you with utter remorse
My libido's subsiding.
You just got through riding
The pony. Don't beat a dead horse.

I approached her and asked, "Who's your friend?"
She said, "Someone who told me to send
You away should I find
You have sex on your mind."
Through this cockblock, I met a dead end.

As my circle jerk party is planned,
I love watching the guest list expand.
Maybe some will come early
For setup. I surely
Would love if they gave me a hand.

Though I saw you two kiss, you're maintaining
Your innocence, sadly explaining,
"He's kin." Kin don't kiss
Quite like that, so don't piss
On my leg and then tell me it's raining.

My old man is a dustman; he picks
Up your rubbish. He found in the mix
Some stilettos, a blouse,
Skirt, and wig at one house.
Now he looks like those street-corner chicks.

"You have dandruff," my skin doctor said,
"Which are skin flakes—large, oily, and dead."
He prescribed some shampoo,
And my social life grew.
Since that day, I've been getting good head.

Said a pirate, "I bought me a cutie,
An overseas whore, and she's duty-
    free; all of her treasures,
    Which give me such pleasures,
Are mine—that's some very fine booty!"

I testified one day in court,
Where I gave an ear-witness report:
    "What I heard weren't the cries
    Right before someone dies;
They were more of the sexual sort."

"For that white creamy filling, I ache.
I love Ding Dongs," she said. My mistake
Was revealing my cock.
In the midst of her shock,
She screamed, "Perv! I meant chocolatey cake!"

"Would you care for some *vin et fromage?*"
I inquired of my dame de voyage.
That's a doll made in France.
Park my car? Here's my chance
In, albeit, a latex garage.

Can't you see that I crave copulation?
Your reticence causes frustration.
I've made myself clear—
Get your butt over here.
Do you need an engraved invitation?

I'm drawn to these flashing red lights
And to what all that blinking invites.
Off and on goes the neon.
It spurs me to be on
The inside and take in the sights.

A hot bookkeeper had to announce
To two fools that she deals with amounts.
"I add and subtract
In a balancing act.
Double-entry pertains to accounts."

I've developed a passion, it's true,
An irrational fondness for you.
There's no rhyme and no reason
For findin' you pleasin'.
I love you, my skank. I just do.

I sought action; this guy sent me here.
No offense, does it look like I'm queer?
He misread my demeanor,
Assumed I like wiener,
And that's why I got a bum steer.

Getting head from identical twins,
Sameness ends, and distinction begins.
I can tell who is who.
Linda hasn't a clue
How to please me; the sex skills are Lynn's.

A virgin was given a toy
For the bedroom. Her friend said, "Enjoy!"
Sighed the virgin, "This dildo
May give me a thrill, though
I've heard it's more fun with a boy."

A man had a passion to diddle;
His wife wanted only a little.
They asked, "What can we do?"
Said their counselor, "You
Two should compromise—meet in the middle."

Wow, that barmaid is buxom! By far,
The most full-bosomed babe in the bar.
Have you noticed her tag
Just above her right bag?
It says "Melanie." Yes, they sure are!

My boyfriend's a ghost. Yes, it's true.
Every night in my bedroom, we screw.
You think *that's* strange? What's heard
Neath the sheets? Not a word.
When he's with me, he doesn't say boo.

"Will Robinson, DANGER! Refrain
From the pleasure you saw us attain!"
Dr. Smith cried, "You face
Certain harm in this place
From the whips and the chains! *Oh, the pain!*"

Crudités, uncooked veggies, I saw
On a tray served with dip, and my jaw
Nearly dropped at the sight
Of the hostess that night.
I thought, "Wish I saw *her* in the raw."

I broke up with my girlfriend. Dissension
Arose; she expressed apprehension
About doing oral.
She found it immoral,
And that was our bone of contention.

This contortionist woman I see
Sure can please to the utmost degree.
She goes out of her way
With our rolls in the hay
When she bends over backwards for me.

Family sang, "Happy Birthday to You."
Then the birthday cake candles I blew
After making a wish
To devour that dish—
Not the cake, but a girl that I knew.

For Santa's amusement, he'll go
To the strip joints. His pleasure will show
When he's getting his jollies
From young, topless dollies
Who lap dance. He'll shout, "Ho! Ho! OHHHH!"

In a castle lived young Mistress Glover
And spouse. He was shocked to discover
A man in his place
With a smile on his face;
In their bed lay the chatelaine's lover.

A condomless roll in the hay
Worried Kay with her menses delay.
She cries out, now unstressed
Since her pregnancy test,
"Boy, I sure dodged a bullet *that* day!"

That woman in sales I adore.
I was sold by a roll on the floor.
Severe censure ensued,
I got canned, again screwed,
And I'm called on the carpet no more.

Asked a hooker approaching my truck,
Which was stopped at a light, "Wanna fuck?
Got some C-notes? Those bills
Make me show my true skills;
You'd be getting more bang for your buck."

That hot dream caused my penis to grow.
When I poked you, I'd no way to know.
The factor beyond
My control was that blonde.
I'm a victim of circumstance, Moe.

You're displaying your tits as men drink,
And they leer. You're hot stuff, so you think.
Most go back to their lives
With their girlfriends and wives,
So don't act like your shit doesn't stink.

Blindly, Oedipus did as was fated.
Killed his dad; with his mother, he mated.
On the latter, this lesson—
Before you go messin'
Around, know you two aren't related.

My bifunctional penis, you see,
Serves two purposes: one is to pee;
Number two is to fuck—
But I've, lately, no luck.
So okay, masturbation—that's three.

Jesus Christ! What the hell were you doing!
You slut! My best friend, you were screwing!
I saw you, in fact,
In the act of the act!
Our love's dead; I was there for the viewing.

"Holy cow! You're a dish! Wanna spoon?"
"That's a laugh. How 'bout fiddling real soon
With my cat? Diddle too.
Be a sport. Then we'll do
Doggie style; you can jump on my moon."

When it comes to our sex life, my bride
Is quite passive; no passion's applied.
She'll participate, yes,
But not actively. Guess
You could say she's along for the ride.

"Are you cheating on me?" my wife cried.
Hanky-panky I firmly denied.
"Why'm I coming home late?
Lots of work fills my plate."
But I've really a bit on the side.

"It looks like you're pitching a tepee.
Drop your drawers. Let me feel that big peepee,"
The urologist said.
But instead I just fled.
I don't strip for no doc who is creepy.

My conservative girl yelled, "We're through!"
When, in bed, I proposed something new.
In thoughts kinky I basked.
"How *could* you," she asked,
"Think that *I'd* do what nice girls don't do?"

One day, I was making the track
To St. Ives, when I met walking back
A wise man, who said, "Son,
The true meaning of fun?
Having pussies galore in the sack!"

I'm no YMCA kind of guy.
Working out? Hell, I won't even try.
Said my girl, "Why not munch
On a scrumptious box lunch?
Let's go down. You can *dine* at the Y."

Said a young, degreed, gay man named Bronson,
"Upon finishing U of Wisconsin,
A sheepskin I got.
Penile Studies was hot.
Now I'll go for my master's in Johnson."

Gathered guests, we're so sorry for this.
We got carried away with our kiss,
Which then led to much more
At the altar. Ignore
What you witnessed—connubial bliss.

The Scarecrow got raked over coals
After sharing with Dorothy goals
Of a sexual theme.
She yelled, nixing his dream,
"Look, I don't elect those with straw poles!"

My phone by my gluteus mass
Aired the fact I'd a lap dance. Alas,
I had butt-dialed my spouse.
My return to our house
Found her kicking me out on my ass.

I went to a mountain lodge dance,
Where I thought I'd advance to romance.
From that night bedding Mia,
Who had gonorrhea,
I caught this damn cold in my pants.

I once was a straight guy pretender
And secretly liked my own gender.
I couldn't come out
Till one night, on a bout
Of binge drinking, I went on a bender.

My banana's own hammock, my thong,
Lets me show off the size of my schlong.
When I lie on the beach,
Passers-by often preach,
As they notice my bulge, "That's just wrong!"

I got head from a pretty Venetian.
First, arousal brought pre-cum secretion.
Intensity built
And, fulfilled to the hilt,
I erupted in breathless completion.

Listen, don't shoot the messenger, dude.
Don't blame *me* for reporting I viewed
Your new bride and best man
In the back of a van.
Yell at *them* for the sex that ensued.

Sneeze? I'm silent. Don't let this depress you.
It's just I'm an atheist. Guess you
Can help me to find
Some religion—the kind
Where we screw and I shout out, "God bless you!"

To the city I drove, zipper down,
With a woman of oral renown.
As I guided our ride,
I went north with great pride
While she also was going to town.

Bob is gay, and he just doesn't see
What bikini-clad babes do for me.
"Most of all, I'm in awe
Of what's *under* the bra,"
I explained. Not ol' Bob's cup of tea.

The Sarge one fine night sucked my flute,
But the brass heard and gave us the boot.
We were ousted, let go;
We received the heave–ho.
Now I give him a civil salute.

My tryout in porn made them sob:
"Oh ... oh ... OH! My God!" "Wow! What a knob!"
"A remarkable willy!"
"A doozy!" "A dilly!"
I, needless to say, got the job.

I brought my best friend to our house.
His black cock was a gift to my spouse.
"Don't tell Kevin," she said,
As they lay in our bed,
"But I really just wanted a grouse."

Try again, dear, tomorrow. All right?
We've been at it so long, but despite
Your not climaxing, Joe,
I have gotten there so
Many times, I'm exhausted. Good night.

A companion's one part of a match,
Or it's one onto whom you attach
Like a pet, friend, or aide,
Or an escort who's paid
To allow you to enter her snatch.

I'm very successful, I am.
I sure scored with a little wham-bam.
Now my teacher's in awe.
Flying colors she saw.
I came through on my entrance exam.

I admit my admittance to Yale
Came through no educational scale.
My acceptance I owe
To the dean. I can go,
I confess, 'cause I gave him some tail.

My dad is a stick-in-the-mud.
Flowing royally blue is my blood.
I'm a nobleman, prince,
Heir apparent. He'd wince
If he knew I get commoner pud.

Lola's blowjobs were much in demand,
But she stopped, and I don't understand
Why she ceased sucking dick.
"Won't you give it a lick?"
I implored. She said, "Talk to the hand."

Bifurcation in utero split
My equipment in two. I admit
It gets crowded down there.
For this reason, I wear
Baggy boxers for looseness of fit.

At prom's end, my date made an admission.
"I've never had sex, though I'm wishin'.
I'm like cars that are new
And unused. What to do?"
She's no longer in cherry condition.

Mary's pregnant with nary a prod
Or a poke from a mortal man's rod.
The Almighty, she claims,
Having infinite aims,
Filled her up with the Spirit of God.

In our course, Better Sex, the instructor
Chose Pam to assist him; he plucked her
Up out of row three
And reminded us we
Should be taking good notes. Then he fucked her.

That took a lot out of me. *Whew!*
Do you mind if I rest for a few?
I'll perk up after getting
My second wind, setting
The stage to go round number two.

Screamed a firm fundamentalist, "Dang!
I have never seen such a huge wang!
Let our bodies collide."
The Earth moved, and she cried
While exploding, "It's true, the big bang!"

At the height of our sexual scene,
For the third time this weekend, "James Dean"
Was the name that she squealed.
"It's not you," she revealed,
"Who I think of. I have to come clean."

Two chicks sized me up at the mall,
When one said to the other, "Too small."
Confused at 6-6,
I then learned they eyed dicks;
They were shopping for baskets. What gall!

Baseball Annies show up in the bars
On the road, causing marital scars
When these groupies, with smiles
And their feminine wiles,
Get to ball with some Major League stars.

"Dan, pornography's nothing but smut.
Cede the point; it's no use to rebut."
The counterpoint made?
"It's a sexual aid.
Oh, and Jane, you're an ignorant slut."

She went to the altar's vicinity
Exclaiming, "I have an affinity
Not only to God
But that hunk, Father Todd!"
And she then offered up her virginity.

Back in college, the women I had
Up at Harvard were not at all bad.
But I must say the Cliffies
Produced way more stiffies.
Those hotties were totally rad.

Veronica sent out a mailer
With hopes men would visit her trailer.
Fifty cents, or four bits,
Lets you feel up her tits.
For a little bit more, you can nail her.

It takes two equilibria, dear.
The receptors of *my* inner ear
That register balance
Don't give me such talents,
So no Kama Sutra, I fear.

In the throes of our passion, there came
To my mouth, brief and sudden, the name
Of my ex. What a mess!
I ejaculate, "Jess!"
When I'm screwing with Tess. Utter shame!

In the fifth, with my extra-base hit,
I reached second. By happenstance, it
Is the self-same locale
Reached that night with a gal
I just met when she gave up some tit.

"Spell feces," I asked of a Brit.
"F-A-E-C-E-S," he said. Writ
On my card was no A.
I said, "No." He yelled, "Hey,
I'm correct! Don't you give me that shit!"

Had to pee, so I used the facilities.
A man, who dispensed with civilities,
Stuck his pole in my stall
Through a hole in the wall.
I then showed him my oral abilities.

Had to pee, so I used the facilities.

"That organization's not free
To get in; it requires a fee,"
Said a chick, who thought, "Hey,
I'll get fellas to pay
For the privilege of entering *me*."

Be careful of parts you expose.
You have cameltoe. Everyone knows.
Lose the spandex. Then maybe a
View of your labia
Outline won't show through your clothes.

"BJ Bonnie ranked high on my roster.
To my horror, I learned this imposter
Turned out to be you,
My own servant. BLECH! EWWW!
No more cross-dressing, Igor!" "Yes, mahster."

A fanny pack's worn on the hips.
It holds money and such, and it zips.
If you're in the UK,
Call it bum bag, okay?
Fanny there denotes "genital lips."

My lovemaking knowledge was none,
But the pro I employed knew a ton.
Just the basics I bought.
Introduction she taught
As she schooled me in Sex 101.

An eccentric man died with a boner.
The organ he willed as a donor
To one who had none.
It changed hands. I'm his son,
Former daughter, and happy new owner.

Hannah hired an odd-jobber to do
Varied tasks round the house, quite a few,
And one more every day
That her husband's away.
She employs him to give her a screw.

"You've one wish for the asking," said she.
"Just request it, and so it shall be."
Now I find she's a meanie.
That hot-looking genie
Refused to get busy with me.

On All Hallows' Eve, in the mix
Of the door-to-door children, some chicks
Who weren't candy-obsessed
Were instead out there dressed
Up like hookers and asking for tricks.

Jack the zookeeper, high off the grape,
Got the notion to bugger an ape.
From his bombed state of mind,
He has sobered to find
An embrace and no way to escape.

Though I've had many women before,
I thought *you'd* be the last I'd adore.
Now I learn that you've been
With a man. That's a sin!
I can't wed one who's fallen, you whore!

"That guy put his hand down the cup
Of your bra and he fondled you?" "Yup.
He's one helluva hunk.
After tickling his junk
At that pool hall, my back got felt up."

A voyeur was admiring the view,
When the woman he eyed hollered, "Shoo!"
Her boyfriend, a true one,
Then ripped him a new one.
Now where is that perv? ICU.

Long ago in the childhood of Man,
Early humankind, cave dweller Dan
Had discovered a tool
That he thought was real cool.
That's the point masturbation began.

A postgraduate once wrote a treatise
About flirting and where it might lead us.
When his fieldwork was done,
He roared, "Boy, was that fun!"
And wrote, *Flirting can lead to coitus.*

My pious ex-bride thought a lot o' me
Till that night when she screamed, "Your life's gotta be
The biggest façade—
A devotion to God
And an interest in practicing sodomy!"

I'm short of a load, a few bricks.
Stupid's something they say you can't fix.
I don't mind I'm not smart.
I've a well-endowed part,
So I never go wanting for chicks.

"I will deal gamers in," explained Trish.
"I include them if that is their wish.
Men will tackle my front
As they line up to hunt
For my G-spot. I call it Go Fish."

I suck in the golf student role,
But my teacher is hot. Thus, my goal
Is to show her I'm good
When it comes to my wood.
I'll try sinking my putz in her hole.

"According to Hoyle, you're wrong.
That is not how to suck on a dong.
See this sex book? Review it.
It tells how to do it
Correctly." She told me, "So long."

"We heard that, onstage, you're a prancer,
A gentlemen's club topless dancer.
Is this true?" "Dad, that's low
And contemptible, so
I won't dignify that with an answer."

"Spread eagle—your legs open wide
And your hands on the wall!" the cop cried.
I assumed the position
With no inhibition
And took his big nightstick inside.

Our son deserved one at the top,
With the medical know-how, no flop
Whose botched jobs are quite scary.
We chose our state's very
Best mohel—the cream of the crop.

Short of breath, with her face getting paler,
My gal plugs away as I nail her.
Despite coughing and wheezing,
She finds the sex pleasing.
When done, she gasps, *"Grab my inhaler!"*

A woman who's been 'round the block
Has experienced multiple cock.
Like that neighborhood hussy
Who isn't too fussy.
Men looking for sex just need knock.

Said a popular hooker named Grace,
"I can't give you a time or a place.
I'm all booked." Then she saw
My huge manhood. In awe,
She screamed, "Wowza! For you, I'll make space!"

The weatherman's forecast? Not right.
"Heavy snowfall," he'd said. It was light.
Claire, the anchor, drew stares
The next day, asking, "Where's
That eight inches you promised last night?"

Bob and Carol and Alice and Ted
Did a mate-sharing four-way in bed.
Though at first they were keen
On the notion, it's seen
Now in hindsight as best left unsaid.

"I like women. It's not that I'm gay,"
I explained, but she just walked away.
Damn ED! On inspection,
She saw no erection
And said, "No hard feelings, okay?"

Her request left me dumbstruck today.
You can't pigeonhole nice girls the way
That I did. She asked, "Honey,
You wanna give cunny …
The cat got your tongue?" *You might say!*

Downtown is where Frosty will go
When traversing the white fields of snow.
He got busted. A cop
Saw him, hollering, "Stop
Going humpity-hump with a ho!"

We were picnicking out in the grove
When she started undressing, by Jove!
Such surprise to these eyes
Quickly gave me a rise,
But my sex drive, alas, overdrove.

I licked her. Her scent? It was fresh.
Soon our eyes met. The feelings of flesh
Upon flesh ruled the night
Till she trashed it outright
When she played a CD of John Tesh.

God said, "Eve is ideal, as I planned."
Adam saw with his own eyes how grand
Was her beauty. He swelled
Down below. This compelled
Him to further behold her first-hand.

Said a guy with a whole lot of moxie,
"Your boyfriend appointed me proxy.
As his fill-in, I'm taking
His place. Let's start making
Sweet love with my much bigger cock. See?"

Swore my date, "Cross my heart, hope to die.
Hand to God, I'm not banging that guy ..."
I was filled with despair
When she didn't stop there.
"... But the truth is, I'd sure like to try!"

A philanthropist gal, Molly Brown,
Loading lifeboats, helped some not to drown.
She had many a cause,
And the least of her flaws?
Said her suitors, she wouldn't go down.

When I wake, I oft notice my hubby
Is semi-erect with a chubby.
When the mood strikes, I'll make
His dick fully awake
Then climb on. Always on. He's a tubby.

I sought fun with my date, who is small—
A slim figure and not very tall.
On her, fun-size looks hot,
But on me, it does not.
She made fun of my junk. "Is that *all?*"

While in Asia, I took the advice
Of some locals. "You can't beat the price
Of a blowjob bar—sucks
For about 20 bucks,
Plus there's beer." So I went and came twice.

"Grody! Gag me," she screamed, "with a spoon!
That's so gross! I'll be vomiting soon!
Just the thought of you two
Having sex is like *Ew!*
Plus, it's still only midafternoon!"

"Could she *be* any duller?" thought Cliff.
But he notices now, with a whiff
Of her scent, an effect
That he didn't expect.
Guess those pheromones work. He's bored stiff.

No debutantes, girls of society,
I date just the garden variety.
The middling, mundane,
Unremarkably plain.
They don't give me performance anxiety.

Extinguished before it began
Was my plan to get busy with Ann,
The town nympho. She shot
Down my notion, "I'm not
Putting out for just any old man."

I had only one scene at the start
Of my movie career. Not so smart,
I once scared off a date
When I happened to state,
"In a porno, I've got a bit part."

Your friend fixed us up on a date.
Introducing us proved to be fate.
There's no romance we share,
But we sure are a pair.
How'd she know that the sex would be great?

Eva Gina sells dresses for prom
On her web site. Defusing a bomb,
When some creeps had stopped by—
Her domain name was why—
She renamed evagina.com.

Men, don't put this one site in your browsers.
It won't give you a rise in your trousers.
I had hoped for hot chicks.
All I got, though, were pix
Of hot *dogs.* Oxymoron? They're bowsers.

While in London, I ordered some chow.
"That cute waitress with sausage is *Wow!*
Man, what *she* has looks great!"
Asked the waiter, "So mate,
Wanna banger?" I answered, "And how!"

My wife says, because I get flirty
In chatrooms with Paula (she's purty!),
It's a cyber affair.
Sure, deep feelings we share,
But it's not like we're doing the dirty.

With fillerish tangents, you hide the point.
Thus, readers are largely denied the point.
Be tight when you write ...
Like that pussy last night.
Sorry, class. Disregard. That's beside the point.

"Does that bulge in your pants near your pocket
Mean you're happy to see me? My socket
Awaits." In no way
Was I gun-shy that day,
So I pumped and went off like a rocket.

Said an old guy while bedding a honey
Not long out of high school, "It's funny.
Sags and wrinkles we get
As we're aging, and yet
I've the body of someone who's twunny."

Hiya! Mosey on over. Guess who
Has their burning bush calling to you.
Honey, give me your milk
With the smoothness of silk.
Let our journey last all the night through.

"We limit donations to ten,"
Said the sperm bank receptionist when
I was leaving. "Goodbye.
See you next time." But I
Have bad hearing. I asked, "Come again?"

Viagra's effect was adverse.
With a four-hour hard-on, my curse,
I sought quick aspiration
Of vessel dilation
And went to go see a head nurse.

Once a wild, screaming banshee in bed,
She's now quiet. Experience led
Her to stifle loud wails
When she came with her males.
Far too many lay instantly dead.

I began my career in hard porn
When a men's room voyeur eyed my horn
And said, "You'd be ideal
In the movies. For real!"
A star, as they say, was then born.

My landlady came to my door
Saying rent was delinquent. I swore
That I'd pay her real soon
When the time's opportune.
Then I settled things up with my whore.

My editor's such a damn prude.
He will bowdlerize content that's viewed
As offensive to him.
I complained, "When you trim
My erotica, readers get screwed!"

A Freudian slip's a mistake
That reveals one's unconscious. Let's take,
For example, my date. Her
Response to the waiter,
Not "ounce," but instead, "Six-*inch* steak."

"Look, Jane, look! Here comes Dick. Let's have fun,"
Sally said, "and let's tease him a ton."
Talking dirty, they got
Dick puffed up a whole lot.
Jane cried, "Sally, see spot! See spot run!"

The candidate gave it a whirl. He
Led most of the way and was surely
A shoo-in. Instead,
Like with chicks in his bed,
He fell victim to peaking too early.

Does my job test my scruples? Yeah, some.
I can cope 'cause the pay's pretty plum,
Plus I fetch hefty tips.
I've come firmly to grips
With the fact I make horny men come.

My guy speaks two languages. One he
Grew up with—that's English. My honey,
Though, learned something new,
And I'm thrilled through and through
That he's also now lingual in cunny.

"My defect gives sex partners shock. I'd
Prefer to get surgery, Doc." "I'd
Be glad to. What's wrong?"
"You can see on my dong
A diagonal pee-hole. It's cockeyed."

Said my gal, "I've been standing all day
At my job. Hon, you sure have a way
With your hands. I could go
For a foot rub. You know ...
You massage and then guess where *I'll* play."

She abruptly inhaled from her shock
At the horror film. Then I took stock
Of her mood. From a hug
And a kiss came a tug
And a *bigger* gasp, eyeing my cock.

When I asked, "Would you care for a wiener?
A footlong?" she beamed. Her demeanor
Was lustful. I made
Her a frank. I'm afraid,
On a 12-inch long dong, she was keener.

In the car repair lobby, she stood
Eyeing Gus, thinking, "Man, he looks good!
I have long been denied.
He could sure fix my ride
In the bedroom by popping my hood."

To the farm from the funny farm, Sam
Had escaped. He was able to scram
And go back to his life
With his four-legged wife.
Men in white soon found Sam on the lam.

"But Kevin, just how do you know
That our sweet, demure classmate's a ho?"
"Live and learn. Once you lay her,
She'll tell you to pay her.
Chalk it up to experience, bro."

"As a rule, if they're weird," said a guy,
"I'd let sexual fantasies lie.
Minds can go far afield
With desires. Keep those sealed
'Less you know your mate's willing to try."

What's my breast size, you ask? Double D.
Just unclasp me, and then you can see.
Don't be shy. Be my guest.
Help yourself to my chest.
Wanna fondle these puppies? Feel free.

I remember when, back in the day,
Like today, in my room I would play
And my mother made use
Of the term *self-abuse*.
Am I dating myself? In a way.

"All was set," said a date auction bidder.
"The sale was approved. I got wid her
And went out for a meal.
That was it—a done deal—
'Cept for later that night I done did her."

Attending a concert one night,
Was a groupie in awestruck delight.
Soon a backstage pass led
To a suite and the bed
Of Keith Moon and a bit of alright.

That gondola ride got our vote.
We shared romance in Venice afloat.
Later on with my gal,
I came down her canal
As I perked up her man in the boat.

I got wind of your secret—the fact
You were doing the sexual act
With my friend. Rumors flew.
Then I learned it was true
From the source; in a restroom, she yakked.

"You're perverted! A good girl, I am!"
Cried the student. Her prof said, "Uh, ma'am?
I don't know what you thought,
But please, don't feel distraught."
He then gave her an oral exam.

"In extracting this long rubber dong,"
Said the doctor, "I knew it was wrong
When I laughed. Sorry, miss.
The inscription on this
Foreign body reads, 'MADE IN HONG KONG.'"

I recall she was pretty and young.
I did cunny; her bell sure got rung.
What's her name? Well, let's see …
Wait. It's coming to me.
She is just on the tip of my tongue.

Did I like LBJ? I did not.
In fact, much from the sixties was rot.
Just one thing I will hail—
My town's overhead rail-
Riding hookers; el BJs I got.

With a chastity belt, she's equipped.
With no chance to have sex, feeling gypped,
I asked, "Why have a locking
Device, thereby blocking
Your beaver?" Who knows? She's close-lipped.

Lying naked and whacking his whang
Was the butler, who suddenly sprang
From his bed with the sound
From the bellpull, came round
Within seconds, and panted, "You rang?"

"Your love-making skill really blows!
This is amateur hour. It shows
In no foreplay, a quick
In-and-out with your dick,"
Whined my date, "and a post-coital doze."

That female magician's pursuing
A change in career. She likes screwing,
So she'll give up the wand
For the johns. She's more fond
Of the new set of tricks she'll be doing.

"My dentist's a hunk!" she thought, thrilling
To fantasies while he was drilling
And fixing her tooth,
After which she said, "Truth
Is my cavity south could use filling!"

Not in school, I am absent today.
My hot teacher is also away.
Coincidence? No.
We decided to go
Have a rollicking roll in the hay.

The woman I'm dating, a fox,
Is an airplane blonde. Gold are her locks,
But she dyes it. The hair
She possesses "down there"
Near her cock pit reveals a black box.

I wished to transcend the mere friend zone.
In my mind, we made love. This pretend zone
Saw light when I threw
You a pass, to which you
Were receptive and ran to the end zone.

"For just $9.95, I will tickle.
Pay 90 bucks more, and your dick'll
Have fun in my loins."
I, without any coins,
Paid a hundred; got sex change—a nickel.

Her disinterest in me I lamented,
Then to intimate sex she consented.
You ask how I succeeded?
I begged and I pleaded
For favors. She finally relented.

There oughta be some kind of law.
It was ample, the chest that I saw.
Back at my place, she slipped
Off her clothes. I felt gypped,
Because falsies had padded her bra.

At a health club with Daddy, I ran
To the locker room, needing the can
For a pee. I checked under
One stall door, and wonder
Of wonders, a four-legged man!

A cop, of the ginger-haired kind,
Sought massages in efforts to find
Whether more could be bought
And, if vice offered, caught
Them red-handed, but never did mind.

I had eyes for that pastry school chick,
So I flirted. Things started to click.
Later on at my place,
She insisted, "The space
Where my pie is needs filling—your dick."

Rick had hits at an earlier age.
Gathered guests scorned his turning the page.
The reaction was rough
When he played newer stuff
And was pleasing himself up on stage.

As the sultan, if I had my way,
I would rather choose you any day
Than the myriad others;
But I don't have my druthers.
With this harem they force me to play.

You're my concubine, darling. Don't grouse.
Though your status is low in this house
And our children aren't heirs,
In our carnal affairs,
You come first. Go downstairs; ask my spouse.

An art fair exhibiter, Nash,
Left his paintings and fled with a dash.
Art's not all he'd present
To a gal in his tent.
The police found the guy in a flash.

"You have something to offer? You say
It's of value? In what kind of way?"
"I can bring to the table
The fact that I'm able
To service your members today."

Prayed a midwife in ages medieval,
"Dear God, we face major upheaval!
The spawn comes from semen
Supplied by a demon.
Deliver this baby from evil!"

More embarrassed I never could be.
Guess my earphone he just didn't see.
"When the Oscars are through,"
I said, "sex—me and you."
Asked De Niro, "You talkin' to me?"

"My boobies? For art's sake, I free 'em.
Too bad you're not near a museum."
"Au contraire, my dear Valerie.
An artmobile (gallery
On wheels) comes to town where I see 'em."

I felt such satisfaction inside.
In a manner of speaking, I died
And I then went to heaven.
"Enjoying this, Kevin?"
She asked. "You're amazing!" I cried.

You look awfully familiar, my sweet.
Come to think of it, didn't we meet
By the curb that one night?
On reflection, I'm right.
I remember … I saved the receipt.

That chick's number? I frequently wrote of it.
Guys in the stalls got a load of it.
They're now met with chagrin
At "This number has been
Disconnected." They sadly make note of it.

"I like chasing the women," said Dallas,
"But I need to feed length to my phallus.
I hook up just right
With my queens in the night.
Just one pill makes me larger—Cialis."

The director has shown us the door.
Now we're not in that film anymore.
We were caught having fun
Where the edits are done.
We're again on the cutting room floor.

"I've a strong inclination above
All the rest," said a hippie, a dove.
"At the top, my desire's
Not for peace or cease-fires.
What I feel like is making some love."

"See that chick over there, Mary Lou?
I've a crush on her big time, I do.
To a major degree
Is her hold over me."
"You and all of us here in this queue."

"All the presents are packed on the sleigh.
Where is Rudolph? He's leading the way."
"His bright nose led him down
To a section downtown.
Check the district with red light display."

"We should get more 'acquainted'? Some nerve!
A big slap in the face you deserve!"
Chastised Eve, quite upset.
"Though we're nude, we've just met.
I don't know you from Adam, you perv!"

Help me please get my jollies and tickle
My fancy. Grab hold of my pickle
And stroke to the height
Of my pleasure, alright?
You should know, though, it comes out a trickle.

"I have Bobby and Jack at the ready,"
Thought Marilyn. "The sex flow is steady.
They're available to me.
I ask, and they do me
Right after I take off my teddy."

"Mrs. Robinson, what are you doing?
Seducing me?" "Yes, I'm pursuing
A man who's much younger.
Come quench my fierce hunger.
This cougar could use a good screwing."

She's top dollar, that hooker named Yount.
She'll allow Europe's nobles to mount,
But she alternates screws.
Every other she'll choose.
She is sure to make each second count.

Bob Jones University

BJU I attended and swore on
A biblically principled core. On
A date I just had,
A guy asked, "You're a grad?
Then you must give great head!" What a moron.

Dear Daughter,

    When I was a lad,
I revealed to a girl what I had.
Things progressed. Then came you
Way too soon. Please don't do
What I did till you're ready.

                 -Love,
                 Dad

KEVIN LUCAS

Kevin Lucas has been writing limericks in earnest since 2006, and to date, has composed over 3,000. He likes to note that not all of them are salacious.

His interest in words and light verse rhyming poetry began at a young age. While growing up he enjoyed playing Scrabble, constructing crossword puzzles for his family, and writing song poems.

Other Works by Kevin Lucas

Beats to the Punch
Puns Upon a Rhyme

A Note from the Publisher

Dear Reader,

Thank you for reading Kevin Lucas' collection, *The Little Blue Book of Limericks.* We feel the best way to show appreciation for an author is by leaving a review. You may do so on any of the following sites:

www.TemptationPress.com
Goodreads.com
Amazon.com
or Kindle.com

Join our mailing list to receive updates on new releases, discounts, bonus content, and other great books from Kevin Lucas and

Or visit us online to sign up at:
http://www.TemptationPress.com